Personal Financial

Management

Personal Financial

MANAGEMENT

VILMA EDGINTON

BorderStone Press, LLC

First American Edition

Personal Financial Management

Author: Vilma Edginton

Published by BorderStone Press, LLC, PO Box 1383, Mountain Home, AR 72654
Dallas, TX / Memphis, TN

www.borderstonepress.com

© 2011 by Vilma Edginton

Supervising editor: Brian Mooney

ISBN: 978-1-936670-40-6

CONTENTS

PERSONAL FINANCIAL PLAN

SECTION 1

PERSONAL FINANCIAL PLAN

Where there is no counsel the people fall,
but in the multitude of counselors there is safety.
—Proverbs 11:14—

HAVING A PERSONAL FINANCIAL PLAN is the key to stability and security in both the short term and long term. An effective plan puts your mind to ease knowing that you have strategies in place for the future. And should unexpected circumstances occur, you can turn implement a thought-out plan objectively and efficiently.

Your personal financial plan is YOUR plan. And while there are going to be many individuals associated with your plan, it is not a plan for anyone else but you. Not your neighbor, a friend or even a family member.

Too often, Christians do not take the time in creating a personal financial plan because they rely on God to do it for them. God will in fact provide financially, but He wants you to do your part too. This means, thinking about goals, career paths, spending, budgets and retirement. You can't expect God to bail you out financially when you have no budget, over spend and are wasteful with your money.

Always remember that God is in charge of all the facets our lives and He will always guide and lead us, even financially. We need to do our part and put God #1 on our priority list. In doing so, God will make sure that our financial plan is met, exceeded or directed as He sees fit.

May the Lord give you the desire of your heart
and make all your plans succeed.
—Psalm 20:4 NKJV—

BEFORE YOU BEGIN YOUR FINANCIAL PLAN, PLEASE TAKE INTO CONSIDERATION THE FOLLOWING TIPS:

- Always put God as #1 on your priority list
- Don't rush in trying to complete any part of the financial plan-pray about it and then think it through
- Be careful with who is giving you advice on financial planning... everyone has their opinion and interests
- Gather as much documents in order to complete each section as effectively as possible
- Find a quiet, non-distracting area when working on your financial plan
- Keep your financial plan in area that is private, yet accessible for you to review frequently.
- Never include social security numbers, passwords or bank account information in the financial plan for security purposes

PRAYER:

Lord, I thank you for always providing for me. Come into my heart and be with me as I complete each section of this personal financial plan. I know that only You can construct a financial plan that is perfect for me and my life. So, I ask you to bless me and lead my financial plan so that it glorifies You and Your Word. Fill my heart with love and gratitude and enrich my mind with vision and wisdom. Amen.

JOURNAL:

Why do I need a financial plan? Who will be impacted by the decisions made in this financial plan? How does creating a financial plan make me feel?

EXERCISES 1-1

What is your objective in creating a financial plan? Analyze why it's important to have a financial plan? Who will be impacted by the decisions made in this financial plan?

PERSONAL MISSION STATEMENT

SECTION 2

PERSONAL MISSION STATEMENT

Let us fix our eyes on Jesus, the author and perfecter of our faith,
who for the joy set before him endured the cross,
scorning its shame and sat down
at the right hand of the throne of God
—Hebrews 12:2 KJV—

A PERSONAL MISSION STATEMENT explains what we are trying to achieve in life. It defines our life goals and objectives in the long term. It adds meaning, reason and clarity to why we do what we do. An effective personal mission statement provides us with clarity and stability so that our decisions in each facet of life, even financial ones, make sense and aligns with our personal mission statement.

Every successful company has a mission statement that defines who they are and what they do. Their mission statement is usually displayed on their website and in the yearly financial report that is distributed to shareholders. Similar to business mission statements, personal mission statements should be a reflection of you, your actions and words.

For examples go to:

http://www.missionstatements.com/personal_mission_statements.html

Go to Franklin Covey's website for tips on creating personal mission statements:

http://www.franklincovey.com/msb/

An effective personal mission statement incorporates different dimensions of life such as: faith, personal growth and development, family, career, education, financial and interests. There is no true length to a mission statement, as long as it fully explains your purpose and intention.

Having a personal mission statement apart of your personal financial plan is important because it justifies your financial decisions (spending, savings, and investments). It also serves as a pillar for when we are confused or frustrated financially and need to remember what we are trying to achieve.

A personal mission statement should reflect a long term journey rather than a quest to achieve an objective in the short term. A personal mission statement should be followed and honored for a lifetime so it should be solid, yet transparent with your actions. You can change your personal mission statement as long as you change. You can add to it, or even edit the statement throughout the years to reflect you and your life.

Be still, and know that I am God
—Psalm 46:10 NKJV—

TIPS TO CONSIDER WHEN CREATING
A PERSONAL MISSION STATEMENT:

- Personal mission statements are personal to you and should reflect you and what you are trying to achieve, nobody else
- Don't rush in trying to complete your personal mission statement-pray about it
- Think long term journey instead of short term objectives
- Avoid creating a mission statement to impress others or even yourself
- Consider different facets of life when creating your personal mission statement
- Focus on the quality of the personal mission statement, not the quantity or length of the personal mission statement
- Feel free to incorporate bible verses
- Personal mission statement can be modified or altered in later years

PRAYER:

Lord, my personal mission in life is always to glorify You. Please come into my heart and give me guidance and wisdom in defining my personal mission statement. Amen.

JOURNAL:

What are the most important components of a personal mission statement to me?

_____

_____

_____

_____

_____

_____

_____

_____

_____

_____

_____

_____

EXERCISES 1-2

Complete a personal mission statement.

_____

_____

_____

_____

_____

_____

_____

_____

_____

_____

_____

_____

_____

_____

_____

_____

_____

_____

GOALS

SECTION 3

GOALS

ALL TOO OFTEN, WHEN considering their financial plan, people forget to include their own goals, and visions. Goals are well thought out visions that are written down to ensure accountability and motivation to the person who made the goals.

> Only those who are able to see their dream
> are able to seize their dream.
> —John C Maxwell—

> Goals that are not written down are merely wishes.
> —Unknown—

There are two different kinds of goals that we will be focusing on:

1) *Short Term Goals*
2) *Long Term Goals*

Both sets of goals should be attainable, assessable/quantitative, and reflective upon your mission statement. Goal setting is not an easy process, and will not be achieved overnight. Although you may similarities or things in common as your friends or people you know, you will have all have your own individual goals to reflect on. Goals are not permanent. Life does not always go according to plan, and it is vital to remain agile to our changing environment, by consistently updating and reviewing your goals, or even creating new ones that may be more applicable to your new situation.

Now we will take a moment to define and break down the main differences between long term and short term goals.

Short term goals should be attainable within a year. They will often be more specific since you want to achieve them in a short time and have your vision close in sight.

Long term goals should be focused for a longer time period of over a year, and may have broader criteria because so much could change in that amount of time, both in the macro environment, and within your personal life. The key is that when the macro or micro environment changes, you must adapt your long term goals to coincide with your new mission and focus.

When creating these goals, it is important to consider the following:

- Be bold, and use these guides to challenge yourself as a Christian, student, leader, and person.
- Be specific for short term goals and more general with long term goals (you will utilize an action plan to execute these broad goals).
- Consistently review your goals and make appropriate adjustments to them based on changes in the environment, or personal mission.
- New goals must be established when old goals are met. Learning is not a destination, but it is a continual journey throughout our life.

Your goals do not need to be focused solely on the topic of finance, but can center around other areas of your life as well; such as spiritually, professionally, academically, socially, or even within your relationships you have with others. There are no limits for goals. The purpose of you writing goals *is not for me*; but they are to challenge **you** and hold **you** accountable to continually work to become the person you strive to be in your mission statement.

Do not base your goals on what other people create, or based on what you may think I *want* to hear. These goals are for YOU, and helping YOU reach your full potential.

As understood even in the Greek culture, they created the word, *arête*, which means: ***Be the best YOU that YOU can be.***

I challenge you to reach your highest potential, and don't wait until tomorrow, but use the gifts that God has given you today, to make a difference, and live your life to the absolute fullest.

PRAYER:

Lord, I thank you for providing me with the gifts and abilities to further your Kingdom. I ask that you guide me when creating these goals, and help me to live a life of purpose, and direction. Amen.

JOURNAL:

What goals have you set in the past? Did you achieve them? Why or why not? How will you choose which goals to set to fulfill your mission statement?

_____

_____

_____

_____

_____

_____

_____

_____

_____

_____

_____

_____

_____

_____

_____

_____

_____

EXERCISES 1-3

Create 5 Short term and 5 long term goals:

_____

_____

_____

_____

_____

_____

_____

_____

ACTION PLAN

SECTION 4

ACTION PLAN

AN ACTION PLAN IS A SEQUENCE of steps that must be taken, or activities that must be performed well, for your goals to be achieved. The basic way to create an action plan is to take each goal, and create a strategy and plan to obtain it; and in the long run, fulfill your mission. You can write down an action plan (most effective), or draw out your action plan through a decision tree, or on an excel spreadsheet.

> It's never too late to be,
> what you might have been.
> —George Eliot—

Your action plan should be realistic, but also challenge you to continue working on your goals, step by step. You must be able to adapt to change, and when things are not going perfectly (as they never do), you must reconsider your action plan, and if necessary, make some changes to keep you on track. Your action plan is not the "End all, be all," but rather a guide to help you take a large goal, and make it attainable by small steps. This action plan will help you determine what you have now, as well as what you need to succeed in the future; such as education, finances, or certain opportunities.

Your action plan should include a timeline for each goal, and you must be committed to staying on schedule. Feel free to give yourself small rewards for achieving small steps in your action plan.

Being disciplined is not solely about the sacrifice, but it also means to recognize that your hard work has paid off, and you are one step closer towards achieving your goal.

Your action plan is for your own benefit, and should not be discouraging or overwhelming, but it should give you a realization to make sure your goals are attainable, and to maintain a clear vision. Your action plan has no set parameters because it is impossible to tell what the future has in store, and we must constantly be making adjustments.

Consider the people, places, and resources around you, whom you can provide assistance to help you achieve your goals. In response to this, it is absolutely vital for you to understand the difference between using people, and allowing them to guide you in this process. As Christians, it is our duty to be ethical and responsible in all we do, even when it is hardest thing to do. We have brothers and sisters in Christ not to use for our own selfish wants and desires, but to help prepare us for the world, and to help further Christ's Kingdom.

There is no limit to what you can achieve, but it is a decision, and discipline to work towards your goals on a daily basis, even when it is hard, and you are not reaping immediate benefits.

PRAYER:

Lord, I thank you for your sacrificial love, and ask that you help me live a life of discipline, and focus all for your glory. I thank you for providing me the people I have in my life, and I ask you help me remember to learn, and grow from these people. Amen.

JOURNAL:

What action steps will you have to set up for each of your goals? Do you have people in your life to help with these? In what capacity?

_____

_____

_____

_____

_____

_____

_____

_____

_____

_____

_____

EXERCISES 1-4

Create a set of action steps for each of your 10 goals. (Short Term/Long Term)

_____

_____

_____

_____

_____

_____

_____

_____

_____

Personal Development

Section 5

PERSONAL DEVELOPMENT

Leadership develops daily, not in a day.
—John C. Maxwell—

WHEN YOU WERE YOUNG, and your parents asked you what you wanted to be when you grow up, how did you respond? An astronaut? The President? A doctor? Almost all of the time, you responded to be a successful and influential person. So why have we strayed away from learning how to develop and be successful to fulfill our dreams? Why have we pushed our dreams aside, and pursued a career that provides an income, but not self fulfillment?

This section is about you, and helping you develop and become the person God has intended, and created you to be. What is the greatest investment you can make? Some may say education, others argue a house, while others believe a family. But why don't we ever invest in ourselves? What makes ourselves so insignificant that we don't work at growing every single day, and every single hour? Imagine the potential we would have if we invested in ourselves every day. Personal development does not happen overnight, so you must commit for the long haul, and recognize the rewards you will have in the future by investing in yourself *today*.

I am a strong advocate for personal and professional development. Success is not a destination, but a continual journey of learning on a daily basis. If you want, or have a desire for success, and are looking for ways to excel as a Christian and leader, you need to be committed to being a lifelong student of continual learning. By reading leadership books and material on success, you are enabling and preparing yourself for a future of success.

MY SUGGESTED PERSONAL/PROFESSIONAL DEVELOPMENT BOOK LIST IS AS FOLLOWS:

- *Rich Dad, Poor Dad*, Robert Kiyosaki
- *The Millionaire Next Door*, Thomas J. Stanley
- *How to Win Friends and Influence People*, Dale Carnegie
- *The Compound Effect*, Darren Hardy
- *Make Today Count*, John Maxwell
- *The 21 Irrefutable Laws of Leadership*, John C Maxwell
- *Leadership 101*, John C Maxwell
- *The 7 Habits of Highly Effective Teens*, Franklin Covey
- *Quiet Strength*, Tony Dungy

What kind of legacy do you want to leave on this earth? What do you want people to remember you by? Many people have given the illustration of legacy through "The Dash," which is a poem that talks about a gravestone. When you look at a person's grave, you see their date of birth, date of death, and the small dash in between; but that small dash represents our entire life on this earth. What do you want your dash to represent? What do you want people to say about you? If you invest in yourself, and personal development, you will learn to lead, and leave a lasting legacy on this earth, and to the people you love.

SKILLS ASSESSMENT:

A good start to personal development is recognizing, and assessing your skills, and natural abilities. Not any leader is the same, and we have been given gifts and talents so we can be unique, and develop as individuals. By analyzing, and assessing your skills, you may be revealed your natural ability to lead, or even a new career plan that God has created you for.

If you are not sure what your skills are, then a skills assessment test will help solve this problem, and uncover your talents/gifts. This will also help you distinguish your strengths and weaknesses, which can help assist you in your job search.

Here are a few respectable websites that will help you identify your skills:

- http://www.careerexplorer.net/aptitude.asp
- http://www.careerkey.org/
- http://www.careercolleges.com/career-assessment-test.jsp

PRAYER:

Lord, I ask that you help me commit my life not only to your will, but to my personal development. Help me see the potential I have, as well as my ability to serve others according to your purpose. I ask that you give me determination, and motivation to continue this mentality of learning not only in my college years, but for the rest of my life. Amen.

JOURNAL:

What legacy do you want to leave? What do you want to be known for? What do you need to work on to motivate yourself to a lifelong process of self development?

_____

_____

_____

_____

_____

_____

_____

_____

_____

_____

_____

_____

_____

EXERCISES 1-5

Define the legacy you want to leave. What will your dash represent?

_____

_____

_____

_____

_____

_____

_____

_____

_____

_____

_____

_____

_____

_____

_____

_____

_____

_____

_____

RÉSUMÉS

SECTION 6

RÉSUMÉS

Each one should use whatever gift he has received to serve others, faithfully administering God's grace in various forms. If anyone speaks, they should do it as one speaking the very words of God. If anyone serves, he should do it with the strength God provides, so that in all things God may be praised through Jesus Christ.
—1 Peter 4:10-11—

A RÉSUMÉ SHOULD GIVE YOUR POTENTIAL employer a snapshot of your current and past professional background, as well as your specific skill sets and *gifts*. The purpose of the résumé is to demonstrate to your employer that your skills and knowledge is relevant for that particular job, and if successful, should provide you with an interview.

A résumé is an intricate part of the job search process, and a vital first step to even being considered. In the past, an employer on average would spend 30 seconds-one minute scanning your résumé; but with the competitive job market we are living in, the average scan is now less than 10 seconds![1]

So what does your résumé do to convince the employer to look a little bit longer, and even consider reading the entire document you worked so hard at?

---

[1] http://www.recareered.com/blog/2011/02/24/career-advice-how-a-personal-branding-statement-can-help-job-seekers/ September 13, 2011.

From a business perspective, you should have three different focuses for your résumé to be ready for any situation:

- A résumé geared towards a specific job
- A résumé for the general field/industry you are interested in
- A general résumé that can be used for virtually any position or industry

From a technical standpoint, there are three main types of résumés:

1. Chronological
2. Functional
3. Combination

The chronological résumé is the most common for college students entering the workforce. It focuses on past experiences, in chronological order to show the employer the most recent work and positions. After the listed date and position, you would provide a brief description of accomplishments and duties that were associated with that position.

The functional résumé is geared to emphasize skills and trades, rather than past experiences. This type is more common when you are transitioning in between jobs, and have a specialized skill that will be valuable to that company/employer. This is also used when you have limited education, and work experience.

The combination résumé is a combination of both the chronological and the functional résumé. This is used when you have an education, but have special skills that will be beneficial to the company. This also provides you with the opportunity to display your achievements in the past, but shows the skills you can provide for the future.

DO'S AND DON'TS OF RÉSUMÉ BUILDING

DO'S:

- Begin with your objective.
- Make sure consistency is used throughout your résumé.
- Your résumé should accent your cover letter and vice-versa.
- Make sure your résumé is organized and easy to read.
- Clearly label different sections with appropriate headings.
- Keep résumé to one page.
- Make sure font is readable, and not too large or small.
- Less is more. Bullet points and sentences are most effective.
- Be honest, and proud of what you have done.
- Highlight special skills (not literally) that the application stated they are looking for, and incorporate your skills into that position.
- Use the industry terms when creating your résumé.

DON'TS:

- Don't include any spelling, grammar or punctuation errors! You will be denied immediately.
- Don't include reference name, but imply that "references are available upon request."
- Don't include GPA unless exceptionally high.
- Don't include any high school information. This makes you seem young, and inexperienced.
- Don't include your age directly.
- Don't include a picture in your résumé unless specifically required.
- Don't use colored ink, or colored paper.
- Don't lie, or exaggerate any qualifications on your résumé. If you get the job, you have to be able to achieve what you promised.

YOUR RÉSUMÉ SHOULD INCLUDE, BUT NOT LIMITED TO:

- Current and past Employment
- RESULTS
- Include specific achievements and growth you were a part of within your job
- Quantitative results and gains are especially important for companies looking for quotas, development and growth.
- Education
- Volunteer Work
- Extracurricular Activities
- Special skills/trades
- Contact Information

PRAYER:

Lord, I know that I am put on earth for a reason, and I want to live a life pleasing to you not only in my daily activities, but also in my vocational life. Please guide my path as I get ready to embark on a journey of finding a job, and furthering your will for my life. Amen.

JOURNAL:

Have you created a résumé before? If so, which type? Did you find it to be useful and effective?

_____

_____

_____

_____

_____

_____

EXERCISES 2-1

Create a chronological résumé, functional résumé, and combination résumé.

COVER LETTERS

SECTION 7

COVER LETTERS

A COVER LETTER IS THE FIRST thing an employer sees when introduced to your résumé, so it needs to look professional, clean and well written. Its function is to convince the reader to read the résumé that accompanies the cover letter. In saying this, there should be absolutely **NO** spelling, grammar or punctuation errors. A cover letter is a clear indication of your writing abilities, as well as a great opportunity for you to sell yourself to an employer and convey your enthusiasm for the position. The cover letter is also a way to leave your contact information with them, for future communication and interactions.

Similar to a résumé, there are three types of cover letters that you would give according to various situations.

1. One general cover letter that would be sent to the company
2. One specific cover letter for an individual who will be reading it
3. One cover letter for a specific job you are applying for with defined qualifications

The *first paragraph* of the cover letter should be your introduction as to who you are, and who you are applying to. Make sure that you are addressing the cover letter to the correct person, with the proper title. If you were referred by someone, you may want to include their name, and explain your connection.

The *second paragraph* should highlight two or three of your strengths that you will later demonstrate in your résumé. Briefly explain your reasoning for applying, and why you want the job. You should also include how you intend to positively contribute to the company and organization.

And the *last paragraph* is your closing, and should provoke the reader to read your résumé, and continue to learn more about you. Remember to thank them for their consideration, and that you look forward to meeting them to learn more about this opportunity. Be honest, gracious and respectful for their time.

PRAYER:

Lord, I thank you for the words to say, and the ability to articulate who I am to an employer. I ask that you guide me throughout this process to stay humble, and recognize your grace and mercy in every situation. Thank you for molding me into the person I am today. Amen.

JOURNAL:

Describe yourself in three words. Which of these qualities would be beneficial for an employer? What qualities/skills would they be looking for? Which skills do you need to work on?

_____

_____

_____

_____

_____

_____

_____

_____

_____

_____

EXERCISES 2-2

Create three different cover letters, one general cover letter to send to a company, one specific letter for the individual who will be reading it, and one specifically for the job you are applying for with the defined qualifications.

NOTE: You don't need to remake all three letters, there will be many similarities, just tailored to the various audience.

BUSINESS CARDS

SECTION 8

BUSINESS CARDS

IN A GLOBAL MARKET AND ECONOMY, it has become more difficult than ever to stand out among the crowd. Employers are in contact with hundreds, and potentially thousands of people every single day, with different names, titles, and duties. This is why it is imperative for you to help contacts, or prospective employers, remember who you are, and why you are trying to connect with them. To help solve this problem, it is essential to have a personal business card.

Business cards are not only useful for organizing contacts, but also for you to appear professional to employers and the workforce. Your business cards can be as simple as including your name, email and phone number; or can be as detailed as including your picture (appropriate to various fields), personal cell phone, or social media sites. It depends on your position, the industry you are penetrating, and where you are at in your job search.

Just remember that the more you have on your business card, the more available you are making yourself, as well as an invitation for the company/organization to get to know who you are, on a more personal basis.

In the diverse, global world we live in, we must recognize that not everyone will have the same views and beliefs as ourselves, and we must be considerate to others' position on religion, politics, or even philosophies on life. As a Christian, it is our duty to spread the Word of God, and further His Kingdom; but I would avoid trying to do that on a business card. You never know if the person you give your card to is of a different religion background, and could potentially even be offended by your belief. As a professional, avoid the use of bible verses on your business cards, unless applying to an organization/company that shares the same outlook.

Business cards are also used the other way, as a way to manage, store, organize and maintain your network of contacts. Keep all your business cards in one place, and you can always refer back to them if you need to touch base with someone, or even if you want to stay connected with them while enduring your interviewing process. If they do not specialize or work in your specific field or industry, maybe they have connections that may be of value to you? Or you could even reach out to them to request that they mentor you while you are growing as a person and young professional.

When purchasing business cards, consider the quantity you are ordering, and remember that you may not hold the same title, position, or even address forever. It may be smart (especially when you are just beginning your vocational career) to begin in small quantities, such as 50.

There are many sites and resources that provide free and "cheap," business cards; but it may be wise to invest into something that reflects who you are as a professional, and the value you can bring to an organization/company. "Cheap" may indicate your work is not of high value, and a prospective client, employer, or contact may take that into consideration during the networking, or even the hiring process.

RESOURCES FOR AFFORDABLE BUSINESS CARDS

- www.vistaprint.com
- www.businesscardsusa.net
- (Or go to an Office Max near you)

PRAYER:

Dear Lord, I thank you for the ability to connect with people, and your emphasis on fellowship. I ask that you be with me, while I connect, and establish a network of people who you have placed in my life, to help guide my path for your plan/purpose. Give me wisdom, and a creative eye to create something that will truthfully represent who I am. Amen.

JOURNAL:

Have you created a business card before? What can you picture, that would represent who you are? What information would you include on your business card? What have you done with business cards in the past? What stands out on them to make you notice, or even keep their card?

_____

_____

_____

_____

_____

_____

_____

_____

_____

_____

_____

EXERCISES 2-3

Go to www.vistaprint.com or other inexpensive websites to purchase business cards, and create your own design mock-up of what your personal card would look like, and include the picture in your exercise.

INTERVIEW

SECTION 9

INTERVIEW

Blessed is the man who perseveres under trial,
because when he has stood the test, he will receive the crown of life
that God has promised to those that love Him.
—James 1:12—

HOW DOES AN INTERVIEW RELATE to personal finance? Well, the interview is the first step to landing your job; and having a job=money, and having money=the need for personal finance. The interview indicates the company's interest in you as a prospective employee, based on your résumé, cover letter and maybe references. Although an interview might seem pretty straightforward, there are three elements/phases to an interview:

1. Pre-Interview
2. Interview
3. Post Interview

PRE-INTERVIEW:

Proper preparation is fundamental for a successful interview. You will not get the job you want by simply showing up for the interview; but there is extensive work and research to do prior to walking into an office.

First off, you need to do thorough research on the company. This will help give you confidence when you enter the room, knowing that you are prepared to answer any question they might send your way. Here are a few things you should research while preparing for your interview.

- If they are a publically traded company, you should look into their financial records, their current and past stock prices/performance, their cash flow sheets, and balance statements.
- You should know who their competitors are, and where they stand in their industry/field.
- You should have a general understanding of their public reputation, and the stakeholder's view, and confidence in the company.
- You should be updated on their current news and events, and if there was any current trades, acquisitions, or mergers.
- You should research the typical salary of the position you are interviewing for within that company, so you are prepared to understand the benefits and compensation.

Secondly, you should know who you will be interviewed by, their proper title, and their position in the company. Print off multiple copies of your cover letter and résumé, just to be prepared. Carry business cards, or any other portfolio, sample work you may want to present if given the opportunity. Think of this interview as your only chance to acquire this position, and you do not want to have regrets of being inadequately prepared.

Interview:

When you enter the interview room, walk in with confidence, and a sense of poise that will create a superior first impression with the interviewer. Smile, look the interviewer in the eyes, and present a strong handshake. Introduce yourself and wait to be seated until instructed. When sitting, maintain good posture, and avoid fidgeting with your fingers, clothing, or other items you may have near you. Speak with assertion, as if you have already won the job. Remember to talk slow, because as an interviewee, you will always talk faster when you are nervous, or on the spot.

NEVER ask about the salary or compensation on the first interview. This reveals to them that your motives are monetary, rather than a commitment to invest yourself and time into the company/organization. However, if they ask you how much you want to get paid during the interview, you should express your open-mindedness, but communicate to them your understanding about the average salary for this position. Remember to not sell yourself short, but also avoid being demanding. An appropriate answer may be that you need time to think about it, and you want to affirm a salary that is realistic for your strengths and demands.

Stay away from any topics relating to religion, ethnicity, or political topics. You will not know where your interviewer stands on these issues, and by avoiding these topics, you can elude from saying anything offensive, or insulting.

WHAT THE INTERVIEWERS
ARE NOT ALLOWED TO ASK BY LAW:

- Your Age
- Your Political status
- Your Religion
- If you have any children

When exiting the interview, shake the interviewer's hand, and thank them for the opportunity for you to share your knowledge, skills, and expertise. If you haven't received one already, ask for their business card to keep for the post-interview phase. It is also appropriate to tell them that you look forward to hearing back from them, which indicates accountability for them to contact you.

Post Interview:

Whether you get the job or not, a hand written thank you note is a must. It shows the employer your understanding of effective follow-up, as well as appreciate the fact that they took the time out of the their busy day to meet with you. Do not add any pressure about the decision making, but allow this thank you note to simply be a token of appreciation and thanks.

PRAYER:

Lord, I thank for you for instilling the confidence in me to approach an interview with confidence, knowing that if it is your will, then you will give me the words to say, and the knowledge of whether or not the job is right for me. Please be with me in these next few years as I decide where to begin my vocational journey. Amen.

JOURNAL:

What gives you confidence? What makes you feel like you are on top of the world? Have you ever kept that mentality upon entering an interview, or important meeting?

_____
_____
_____
_____
_____
_____
_____
_____

EXERCISES 2-4

Practice a mock job interview with someone who would be willing to help you through the process, as well as give you constructive criticism and praise. Write a 200-300 word reflection on your experience, and what you learned.

NEGOTIATIONS

SECTION 10

NEGOTIATIONS

YOU ARE ENTERING the experienced work force, it may seem intimidating to negotiate a salary, and discussing potential compensation packages. Remember, you deserve to receive compensation given your skills and expertise.

The number one rule of negotiating with an employer is that you always want the company to reveal the first offer price, so you have something to work with, and can create a counteroffer, and compromise. As with most salespersons, the employer will most likely not give you the highest offer the first time, to give them room for negotiation. In saying this, you need to be smart about your response, to avoid giving the impression of greed, or entitlement.

If the company offers you something significant lower than what is average, you must keep in mind what you must earn to maintain your lifestyle, and enough funds to pay your bills, loans and expenses. Just remember that what you and your employer agree upon (salary, benefits, official title), is a contract; and it is important to wage all your options before signing on the dotted line.

Here are some helpful resources to give you an idea about the salary associated in your designated field of study.

National Association of Colleges and Employers:

They conduct a survey across the United States, relating to new college graduates, and they show what the average salary is, based on the student's field of study.

http://www.naceweb.org/home.aspx

Comp Analyst:

Includes information for college students, and young professionals, who have obtained degrees, as well as work experience within their industry. This includes geographic information, and illustrates what areas of the country make in comparison to other areas. This also breaks the information down to states and cities, to help you understand the average salaries in your local geographic area.

http://www.salary.com/enterprise/
layoutscripts/entl_companalyst_landing.asp

World at Work:

(Used to be called American Compensation Association) Organization that conducts a lot of salary surveys from Human Resources Departments. As an HR department, they enter salary information for employees within various fields, to contribute to the average of the nation.

http://www.worldatwork.org/waw/seminars/html/seminars-compman.jsp

What you can try to negotiate for:

- Vacation time
- Signing Bonus
- Electronic Devices (EX: Cell Phone, laptops, iPad)
- Meal Plans
- Flexible work hours

Don'ts:

- Jump to compensation/salary. Try to wait until the very end of the interview process. You want them to make the first move.
- Give the company your "minimum," of what it will cost to get you to work for them.

P RAYER :

Lord, give me the discipline to avoid greed and materialistic treasures when going through this process. I ask that you give me wisdom when making decisions, and constantly reminding me where these earthly treasures came from, and whose they truly are. Amen.

J OURNAL :

Have you had any experience in negotiations? Did you receive what you wanted? What tactics did you use? Did you keep a biblical perspective when asking for more? How much is too much?

_____

_____

_____

_____

_____

_____

_____

_____

_____

E XERCISES 2-5

Go to http://www.naceweb.org/home.aspx (NACE website) to find out what your projected vocational compensation will be. Is it what you expected? Why/why not?

NETWORKING

SECTION 11

NETWORKING

Be wise in the way you act towards outsiders;
make the most of every opportunity.
Let your conversation be always full of grace,
seasoned with salt.
—Colossians 4:5-6—

NETWORKING IS KEY TO FINDING a career within your passion, skills and desires; especially in this economy. Networking is finding connections with other people or affiliations, and developing a relationship of trust; which could potentially lead to an opportunity in the work force. Networking is completely up to you, no one can network for you. People can introduce you to someone in particular, but then it is in your control to maintain that contact, and follow up with them if necessary.

Here are some important networking tips:

1. Keep in mind that networking is about being genuine and authentic, building trust and relationships, and seeing how you can help others. Don't have selfish motives; think about how you can help them as well.

2. Define what your goals are in participating in networking meetings so that you will pick groups that will help you get what you are looking for.

3. Most networking events have drinks and light appetizers. It is important to recognize that if you are holding a drink, hold it in your left hand to avoid shaking someone's hand with a cold, wet hand.

4. Introduce yourself with a firm handshake, while looking the other person in the eye.

5. To figure out which group of people would be beneficial to network with, visit as many groups as possible that spark your interest. Notice the tone and attitude of the group. Does the leadership appear competent?

6. If you are serious about working for a company, or interning; you may need to hold a volunteer position first.

7. During the actual conversations, ask open-ended questions to maintain the flow of conversation. This form of questioning opens up the discussion and shows listeners that you are interested in them. Maintain good eye contact throughout conversation.

8. Prepare an "elevator speech," in which you can introduce yourself, what you are about, and what you want to do in less than 30 seconds. Have a clear understanding of what you do and why, for whom, and what makes it special or different from others doing the same thing.

9. *Follow through is key*! Make sure you follow up quickly and efficiently on referrals you are given. When people give you referrals, your actions are a reflection on them, as well as yourself. Respect and honor that and your referrals will grow. At the end of conversation, make sure to get business card or way for future contact, and connection.

Networking can take place in a classroom, at church, at work, social events, or at professional events that are sponsored by groups such as (and not limited to):

- The Chamber of Commerce
- Industry Associations (Specific to a particular industry)
- Professional Groups

- Business and Professional Women's Group (BPW)

As I'm sure you are familiar with, social media sites are also a resource that is becoming more popular, and widely used in the professional world. Some of the sites include (but not limited to):

- Facebook
- LinkedIn
- Twitter
- YouTube

The important piece to realize is that although they are entitled as "social" sites, professionals still use them to find out what kind of person you are, and what core values you display. Make sure that you manage your privacy settings, and do not post anything that you wouldn't want a future employer to see, and be impressed by. And always remember that when something is posted onto the internet, it will *always* be on the internet.

Utilize these sites and resources as an avenue to connect with people, but to also spread a positive message. You are living at a time where you can reach and connect with people around the world, so it is up to you to control what message you want to send, and what type of influence you want to create.

By the time you finish this book, you will hopefully realize the value in making connections, and making a lasting impression with people; because you never know who they might be, or how they may help you in the future.

PRAYER:

Dear Lord, I thank you for giving me the self control, and composure to interact with others, on a personal and professional level. I ask that as I begin experiencing these events, that you give me the words to say, and allow me to be a steward of your Word, and love. Thank you God, for your continual blessings in my life. Amen.

JOURNAL:

Have you ever been to a networking event? If so, how was your experience? Were you intimidated? Did you have an elevator speech? What did you gain? What do you wish you would have done better?

_____
_____
_____
_____
_____
_____
_____
_____
_____
_____
_____

EXERCISES 3-1

Create a list of all of your potential contacts that would be beneficial in the field of your pursued career. Re-connect with them to touch base, and reintroduce yourself. Additionally, research networking events in your local area to attend, and list them in this section, and your plan for preparing for it.

COMPANY RESEARCH

SECTION 12

COMPANY RESEARCH

We want each of you to show this same diligence to the very end, so
that what you hope for may be fully realized.
—Hebrews 6:11—

BEFORE YOU BEGIN THE INTERVIEW process, or even constructing a
résumé customized for a particular position, it is essential to do some
thorough research on the company, to determine if you truly want to
work for them. During this time, it gives you an opportunity to explore
specific companies that you think you want to work for, and look deeper
than simply how they are performing in the stock market, and how much
they pay. It is important to look at their mission statement, their code of
ethics, and even their strategic plan to understand their vision for the
future years to come.

To begin this researching phase, start at their website and look for a
vast amount of information. These are a few of the things you should look
for:

- Financial statements, including their balance sheet, cash flow,
  and even past stock performances (especially important if
  applying for financial position).
- Compare the company to the whole industry; who they're
  competing against, and where they stand in the market.
- It also would be effective and useful to search the headlines to
  find out what the company reputation is.

- What is the business culture? Where will you fit in among the mix?
- What is the company's view on social responsibility? Does that coincide with your views?

A company's leadership personnel also represents the success of the company, and where it is heading to. You should look at their board of directors, and find out what their affiliation is, if they are in the same industry, their past successes/failures, and their plans for growth. Are these the kind of people you want to work for, and look to for leadership? Find out where the headquarters are, and if you would be required to move and relocate. Also look at the salary range for the position you are applying for.

You are researching your future, so take your time and make sure to be thorough and not settle for something that collides with what you believe in and stand for. After all, you are committing to working there, and they are investing in you to prepare you to succeed in their environment.

ADDITIONAL RESOURCES FOR RESEARCH TOOLS

- Find reputation about business or an individual:
  www.reputation.com

- 100 Best Companies to work for at Fortune Magazine:
  http://money.cnn.com/magazines/fortune/bestcompanies/2011/full_list/

- 15 Best Companies to Work for at Forbes:
  http://www.forbes.com/2010/12/14/best-places-to-work-employee-satisfaction-leadership-careers-survey.html

P RAYER:

Dear Lord, I ask that while I am searching for your will, my eyes are opened to what you have in store for me. Please be with me during this research stage, and make it clear where you want me to use my gifts you have so graciously given me. Amen.

J OURNAL:

What type of company would you like to work for? How much do you know about them? Have you ever done any research on them? What is their reputation outside of the internal company/personnel?

_____
_____
_____
_____
_____
_____
_____
_____
_____
_____
_____

E XERCISES 3-2

Write a 200-300 word analysis from your company research. What did you find? Did this research reiterate your desire to work for them? Why/why not?

INSURANCE

SECTION 13

INSURANCE

INSURANCE IS THE PROTECTION against financial loss. Insurance is commonly used in every business, or personal life; insurance is everywhere! But there are four main insurances that we will look at in more depth are:

1. Property Insurance: houses, furniture, clothing, computers, other personal property
2. Health Insurance
3. Life Insurance
4. Automobile Insurance

But who should have these? Which plan is right for you? It is evident that you should have car insurance, health insurance, and home owner's insurance; because the potential losses could be detrimental to your finances and even wellbeing.

PROPERTY INSURANCE

It is vital you purchase a good home owner's insurance plan, because they usually not only cover your actual home, but your personal property, for your hotel room if you lost your home (or were unable to live in it), or even personal liability coverage for home injury. When you rent an apartment, or buy a home, an easy way to keep track of your personal property/possessions is to take a video camera, and tour your home (or apartment), documenting all you have in case of a fire, or other disaster. Then take the disc and put it in a safety deposit box at the bank. This is an easy way to ensure your coverage will have a full account of your belongings and valuables; while giving yourself evidence in case you need proof after a disaster.

No matter what your living situation is (renter or home-owner), there is an insurance option for you. There is also renter's insurance, which also covers personal property. This is an option, and you do not *have* to purchase renter's insurance, but understand that most building insurance plans do not cover personal property; so if your apartment complex burnt down, and your possessions were destroyed, you would not be covered under the owner's building insurance.

HEALTH INSURANCE

We are all human. God has made us to have a limited time on this earth. With this being said, we all grow old, our health deteriorates, and we eventually join Jesus in Heaven. But health insurance helps pay for our bills while we **are** here, to prevent sickness from taking us too soon, and giving us the proper treatment we need. Some people risk not having any health insurance, but when something substantial happens to them or their health; they are given an enormous bill that would have been avoided by purchase of health insurance. There are different types of health insurance, with different options and deductibles in each.

It is important to choose a health insurance that is right for you, because your vision and dental are usually included in your health insurance plan if you request it to be.

LIFE INSURANCE

This type of insurance is only necessary when you have dependants still in your family that rely on your source of income to survive. By purchasing life insurance, you are leaving money to your loved ones left behind, while assisting them in paying for the funeral costs, or other expenses that may bring them financial burden. Life insurance also can be used for paying off debt, mortgages, or taxes, education or future expenses for children.

Understand that if you do not have any dependents, or have saved enough money; it may not be necessary to purchase a life insurance policy. An easy way to test if you need life insurance is to ask: "If I were to die, would my death create financial hardship for my loved ones?" If the answer is yes, then life insurance might be a good option to consider.

AUTOMOBILE INSURANCE

Under the financial responsibility law, as a driver, you must prove your ability to cover the cost of damage or injury caused by an automobile accident (i.e. automobile insurance). This was created because of the strong evidence leading to the financial hardship people were experiencing through motor vehicle accidents. Every year, motor vehicle crashes cost over $150 billion in medical costs, loss of transportation, and lost wages; and this is not even including alcohol related accidents.

There are two types of automobile property damage coverage:

- **Collision Insurance**—This insurance covers the damage of an automobile regardless of whose fault the accident stemmed from.
- **Comprehensive Physical Damage**—This type of automobile insurance covers you from the risk of a fire, theft, glass breakage, vandalism, natural causes (wind, hail, flood, lightning, earthquake, avalanche, and tornado) or damage caused by hitting an animal.
  - o Only pays for costs associated to your vehicle (may exclude sound system), and does not matter whose fault.

Insurance is a complicated subject, and it is important to learn more about health insurance, car insurance, life insurance and home owner's insurance; so that you know what is in the "fine print," and how to pick a policy that is right for you, and creates the highest benefits for your individual situation. Be sure to note that insurance policies vary depending on the different states. It is important that you research each policy efficient and choose the BEST for you.

PRAYER:

Lord, I thank you for my time on this earth, and the many gifts you have provided. And Lord, I ask that when I research all of these insurance policies that you reveal to me what the best option is. Lord, I know that you will always provide, and I thank you for that. Please continually watch over me, and under your grace, I am confident in your future for my life. Amen.

JOURNAL:

What insurance do you have now? What do you foresee yourself purchasing when you are out of school? What is important to you? What insurance policies are right for you?

_____

_____

_____

_____

_____

_____

_____

_____

_____

_____

_____

EXERCISES 3-3

Research two health care insurance providers, two automotive insurance companies and two life insurance companies. Compare and contrast the pros and cons. (200-300 Words)

RETIREMENT

SECTION 14

RETIREMENT

A wise man thinks ahead; a fool doesn't, and even brags about it.
—Proverbs 13:16—

WHETHER YOU REALIZE IT OR NOT, everyone has a retirement plan. When you first enter the workforce, you will probably be in your late teens to early twenties. And, you will then work for 35 to 45 years at which time you will be in your mid/late fifties to early/mid sixties. At that point, you may have the option to consider retiring from your job and living off the money you put away throughout your working life and possibly along with monies from your employer (pension) and the Federal government (Social Security).

However, oftentimes retirement seems so far away that when you first enter the workforce, you don't bother to begin saving for retirement. As I mentioned earlier, everyone has a retirement plan and for the person that doesn't begin to save for retirement as early as they can (if even at all), their retirement plan may end up being having to work for the rest of their life because they don't have enough sources of income to afford to retire and pursue whatever interests they may have. Further, employers are tending to eliminate the costly traditional defined benefit pension plans and substitute less expensive defined contribution plans that place the responsibility on the employee to save more for retirement. In addition, Social Security may end up being less generous 35 to 45 years from now as the Federal government is looking to reduce budget deficits be scaling back entitlement programs like Social Security.

With all that being said, I want you to repeat after me your new Retirement Plan *mantra*: "Save as much as you can, as early as you can," by taking full advantage of employer sponsored savings/retirement plans and any other tax advantaged retirement plans you may be eligible for outside of your employer plans.

First of all, you want to consider fully participating in any tax advantaged retirement/savings programs (i.e. a 401k plan or similar type plan) that your employer may offer as soon as you begin working. Oftentimes, your contributions to these savings plans are tax deductible (you get a tax deduction for the amount of your savings contributions) and oftentimes all or a portion of your savings contribution is matched at 50% to 100% by your employer. If you don't take advantage of a plan like this, you are literally leaving money on the floor and walking away from it!!! You should strive to save at least the amount to get the maximum company match and then consider saving beyond that, if the plan allows, to get further tax deductions for your savings contribution. Further, plans like this allow you to defer paying any income taxes on the matching contributions and investment gains until you withdraw the monies in retirement (when you are often in a lower tax bracket).

Then, after fully funding this type of retirement/savings plan, consider fully funding retirement plans outside of your employer's plan(s) like a Roth IRA Plan. You won't get a current tax deduction for the amount you put into a Roth IRA retirement plan, but the amounts (your contributions and investment earnings) you withdraw from it in your retirement years will be free from income taxation under current federal tax laws.

Lastly, as your career takes off and you begin to earn a larger salary thru promotions, merit increases, bonuses, etc., you should increase your contributions to your various retirement savings plans (up to the extent allowed by law).

If you follow these simple steps, when you are eligible for retirement, you should have accumulated enough financial resources to be able to retire and leave the workforce and live a lifestyle that allows you to follow pursue whatever interests you have without having to worry about earning an income, as you will be able to live off of your retirement savings. And, if your employer still has some type of pension plan and Social Security still exists in some reduced form, which will just be icing on your financial cake!

PRAYER:

Lord, I thank you for employers that provide opportunities and funds for retirement. I ask that you help me be diligent in saving for my future, and utilized my employer programs. I thank you for my future retirement, and for your guidance along the way. Amen.

JOURNAL:

What are your hobbies? If you didn't have to work, what would you do? These are the activities that will be possible it/when you retire. What do you know about the various fully funding retirement plans? What would fit your circumstances and lifestyle?

_____

_____

_____

_____

_____

_____

_____

_____

_____

_____

_____

EXERCISES 3-4

What retirement fund/program seems suitable for you? How much will you need to save to provide a retirement fund that will last you for the rest of your life?

LOANS

SECTION 15

LOANS

The wicked borrows but does not pay back,
but the righteous is generous and gives.
—Psalm 37:21—

FROM A BIBLICAL PERSPECTIVE, IT IS recommended to be the lender rather than the borrower, but in some cases, loans are essential to earn an education, or to be able to pay for something valuable. There is this pre-conceived notion that everyone has debt, but this is simply not the case. For some individuals, loans are not needed; and they are able to pay for college, and other expenses, debt free, out of pocket; based on planning, and sacrificial saving. If this is not you, do not worry; just understand the essence of a loan; and what it entails.

A loan is simply a way to borrow money that you do not possess; with the intention to pay it back to the lender. Loans usually require you to pay it back in full, with additional interest to be paid upon the principle. There are many different kinds of loans, such as student loans, car loans, mortgages, home improvement loans, personal loans and more. No matter what you are borrowing for, you **HAVE** to pay the loan back.

Loans appreciate over time, and if you are not careful, you could end up paying more in interest than principle.

For example: if a student took out $100,000 in loans at a 10% Annual Percentage rate (APR) to be paid back in 10 years, they would end up paying $58,520 in interest alone, making their debt of $158,520; before they are even 32 years old.

Some have determined that various loans are "good," while others are "bad." The difference is mainly what you are borrowing the money for. Your student loans for education or your mortgage may be considered "good" loans, because they are an investment; whereas credit card loans and new-car loans are considered "bad," because you are borrowing money for things you want and desire, rather than need.

There are some strategies to pay back loans that you should think about: Should you pay off the smallest loan first; or the largest? Remember that you should **always** pay off the loan that yields the highest interest rates, to be able to pay off the actual *principle*, and not *just* the interest. In the end, by strategically planning how to pay back your debts, you can save money off of interest, as well as reduce stress that links with debt.

There is a lot to remember when deciding about loan options, and it is crucial that you take your time when searching for the loan that best fits your situation and needs. Shop around, and research for the lowest interest rates. Remember that all loans **MUST** be paid back, and if you don't plan, and make a commitment to pay off the loan as a top priority; then the loans can end up driving you in the poverty cycle. When researching these loans, there will be a lot of financial "lingo," that you may need to know, particularly when dealing with the interest rates.

TYPES OF INTEREST

<u>**Simple Interest**</u> is the interest composed on principal only and without ever compounding. It is a fixed rate.

Principal * Interest Rate * Time = Simple Interest

<u>**Add-On Interest**</u> is calculated on the principal amount in full. The interest is immediately added onto the principal, and the payments are

determined by dividing the total (principal + interest) by the number of payments made.

EX: If your interest ends up being $75, then no matter how fast you are making payments, your interest payment will always be $75.

Be realistic about your loan and thoroughly weigh the pros and cons; as well as the tradeoffs. Ask yourself if it is truly worth it. For example:

- If you take out a $125,000 loan for education, but are planning to work at a company that pays only $15,000 a year; maybe you should reconsider paying this much for your education.
- Or, if you take out a loan to purchase a $2,000 suit to interview for a job paying $16,000 a year; is it worth the stress and expense?

Another type of loan that we rarely hear about is the loan from a family or friend. As a borrower, you should treat this loan as though you are borrowing from the bank; and respect their rate of interest, term and qualifications. It should be constructed like an official loan, and although they have a personal relationship to you; you could damage or ruin a relationship if you take advantage of their trust.

—

Go to this site to learn more about loans among family members, and the implications that may arise:

http://www.smartmoney.com/borrow/debt-stategies/loans-among-family-members-9654/

—

Loans can create instability if they are not paid back. They can hold you down, and hinder your ability to live a life doing the things you love. If you are able, I would advise you to pay them back as soon as possible, even if you are paying over the monthly minimum; just to avoid the interest you would pay by paying the loan off until its maturity. And the faster you pay off your debt, the faster you have the freedom to live a debt free life.

PRAYER:

Lord, I thank you for allowing me to earn an education, but I ask that you guide my path when searching for a loan, or paying off a debt. Remind me to have the discipline to pay back my debts, and make it a priority to keep it from controlling my life. Thank you Lord for your daily gifts and blessings. Amen.

JOURNAL:

What kinds of loans do you expect having to take? How much will you have in the next five years?

_____

_____

_____

_____

_____

_____

_____

_____

_____

_____

_____

_____

EXERCISES 5-1

What loans have you taken out? What was the interest rate? What is your plan to pay off these debts in the most strategic way?

SAVINGS AND SPENDING

SECTION 16

SAVINGS AND SPENDING

Be shepherds of God's flock that is under your care, serving as overseers-not because you must, but because you are willing, as God wants you to be; not greedy for money, but eager to serve; not lording it over those entrusted to you, but being examples to the flock. And when the Chief Shepherd appears, you will receive the crown of glory that will never fade away.
—1 Peter 5:2-4—

IF THERE IS ONE THING YOU SHOULD never forget, it is to save as much as you can, as fast as you can, as early as you can, as long as you possibly can! Through the book, "The Compound Effect," Darren Hardy talks about the phenomenon of compound interest, and the astounding return it gives you financially, whether you use it positively or negatively. His mentality is that every dollar you spend, you are actually spending $5, because of the opportunity cost you lose when you spend, rather than invest and save. This will give you a different perspective when buying a "$20" latte every day.

Often times, we forget to recognize how fast the "small things," add up. For example, for that delicious, warm, hot caramel mocha that you *must* buy at Starbucks five times a week for $4; adds up to over $1,000 a year! Or if you go out to lunch every day during your summer job for four months, and kept it under $10 (with tip included), it would still cost you $800. Imagine what you could save by making your own drinks in the morning, and packing a lunch?

The average American saves less than 5% of their disposable income, with most citizens living paycheck to paycheck without any investment into their financial future.

SPENDING LOG

An effective exercise to monitor what you are spending your money on is to log all of your purchases; no matter how small. This will also help put your purchases into perspective, and make you think about it before handing over your credit/debit card. When you have to take the time to log it into your notebook, you may decide that the purchase may be unnecessary and excessive. When you are living on your own, paying bills and have a complex budget, an easy way to monitor your spending is by analyzing your income statement, balance sheet and cash flow. After reviewing these important documents, take the time to highlight what you feel are unnecessary purchases, and become aware, and disciplined to avoid these spending habits in the future.

The key to saving money no matter what your income may be is to, "LIVE BELOW YOUR MEANS." As your professor and mentor, I challenge you to commit to a minimum of 10% of what you make to go directly to savings, but I have high hopes of you being able to save 15-20% of your income to savings if you are diligent, and willing to make sacrifices. Just because the celebrities live a lavish lifestyle of spending, spending and spending; it does not give us the obligation to live a life as they do. Although some magazines highlight the top dollar purchases of celebrities, some of the wealthiest people on the face of the earth have a different view.

According to *The Millionaire Next Door*, most millionaires drive older or used automobiles; mainly for the fact that once you drive a new car out of the lot, it depreciates 30% in value, because it is now considered a used car. Warren Buffet, third richest person in the entire world, who has a net worth of $47 Billion[2], has **never bought a new car**. He believes in the return the stock market can give rather a new car. His view is to "let someone else take the depreciation of the new vehicle," and buy a used car that is only two years old, and drive it until it dies. Some say this seems cheap, considering the fact that he is worth billions; but he *is* wealthy because he didn't spend his money on fruitless investments (such as new cars).

There are a few different savings accounts that are wise to set up, to ensure your plan to allocate your savings for various funds. This may include your "rainy day account," where you do not touch the savings account unless there is an emergency or unexpected event. You can set up savings accounts for your education (or your children's education), or you savings for when you get married and begin a family, or a savings account for when you decide to buy a new car or home. These savings plans are different than retirement, specifically that retirement accounts are normally set up through your employer, and they may have specific incentive plans to invest in a 401K through their company. Many people ask how much is too much to save or spend, and the easiest way to answer this is to live below your means, while still enjoying the time you have with your family and other loved ones.

In an ideal world we would save all of our money so we can retire early, travel the world, and buy a winter home in Florida; in reality there are fixed expenses that we must pay for first, before we pay ourselves. Fixed costs may include your monthly rent, your car payments, cell phone bills, cable/internet bill, utilities and more (assuming they are the same amount each month).

Spontaneous spending has contributed considerably to why Americans rarely save, and spend almost all of their paycheck. Think about the world we live in; think about how much marketers and sales people tell us we

---

[2]http://www.forbes.com/lists/2008/10/billionaires08_Warren-Buffett_COR3.html September 17, 2011.

need. The average American is exposed to 5,000 advertisements a day, each claiming to have the solution to all your problems and worries.

"Need to lose a few pounds? I have the perfect solution... "

"Need more money? Here is a quick way to earn $50,000 a year, while working from home!"

"Want to succeed at your job? Buy these clothes..."

"Need more energy to get more done in a single day? Here is your quick fix..."

All of these advertisements send the same message: You are **not** who you could potentially be, so simply buy this to fix your problems, and help you reach your full potential! The truth is, these ads want you to believe that your wants and desires, are needs and necessities in your life; and you cannot live another minute without it.

A way that you can develop a discipline for saving money is when you are getting ready to spend money, ask yourself if you like it or love it? And do you absolutely need it? If you hesitate at all, you should put the item back, and demonstrate your ability to save, and reap the rewards in the future.

PRAYER:

Lord, please guard my heart and eyes to what I see in our world; and help me be diligent in my savings and spending. Lord, I ask that you continually allow me to control my spending, and desire for money, and to remind me that all these earthly treasures are yours, and I must be a good steward of my money. Amen.

JOURNAL:

Do you have a savings account? What do you use it for?

Do you have a plan for your spending and savings? How can you improve your savings disciplines?

_____

_____

_____

_____

_____

_____

_____

_____

_____

_____

_____

EXERCISES 5-2

Create a spending log, and for this week, log everything you spend your money on; even the smallest items.* What have you learned about yourself?

Include an income statement, balance sheet, and personal cash flow.

BUDGET

SECTION 17

BUDGET

Without consultation, plans are frustrated,
but with many counselors, they succeed.
—Proverbs 15:22—

HOW DO YOU KNOW WHERE YOU are going if you do not have a plan, or an end in mind? This is the same idea with a budget; it is an absolutely essential component in a personal finance plan. In order to save effectively and efficiently, we need to recognize where we are financially, and what we need to change to save and invest. When asked, some people respond that they have a budget in their mind, because they know what they make, and how much they have to save to pay the bills; but this is false...you MUST have your budget on paper. Written budgets set a structure for spending and saving, and you can avoid spontaneous spending when you have a plan and commitment to how you will spend your money. You can make your budget on an excel file, or any place you can store your file, and have it easily accessible to revisit it regularly.

Through a budget, you are given more opportunities to spend, and an enjoyment knowing you have the funds allocated in your budget for that particular expenditure. An easy way to manage spontaneous spending is to ask yourself if you absolutely *need* the item you are thinking of buying. If you are a Starbucks addict, that is okay; just make sure you have a set place in your budget to track this expense. If you love to buy shoes, that is okay; as long as you prepare for the expense in your budget. This allows you to organize and control your spending, while still enjoying the fulfillment of your caffeine addiction. A budget is not created to restrict you, but to help you plan for it.

When creating your budget, remember the rule of saving 10% (as a minimum), before you decide how you want to allocate the rest of your money after expenses.

Here is a sample annual budget of what a **college student's budget** *may* look like:

MONTHLY BUDGET

Expenses:	Amount
Gifts for Holidays/Birthdays	$1,200
Student Books	$1,000
Professional Supplies (Business Cards, etc.)	$100
Entertainment	$600
Bills	$1,000
Groceries	$250
Personal Shopping	$2,000
Savings Account	$695
TOTAL EXPENSES	**$6,745**

Sources of Income	Amount
Summer Jobs	$3,000
On-Campus Job (Part-Time)	$300
Interest on Investments	$650
Scholarship Programs	$3,000
TOTAL INCOME	**$6,950**

ANOTHER EXAMPLE FOR MONTHLY BUDGET

Income/Month	$2,000
Rent/Mortgage	$600
Heat	$60
Electric	$90
Phone/ Internet	$68
Groceries	$400
Car Payment	$100
Credit Card Payment	$100
Savings	$400
Insurance (Car)	$50
Insurance (Home)	$65
Medical Expenses	$40
Left over Funds	**$27.00**

Remember that life never plays out according to plan, and circumstances may show up (Job loss, lower income, new addition to family); and it is your responsibility to be agile, and adjust accordingly.

PRAYER:

Dear Lord, I ask that you give me wisdom, and guidance when developing my budget. I ask that you be with me, and give me self control to commit, and persist to following through with my plan. Thank you for always providing, and for your blessings upon my life. Amen.

JOURNAL:

Do you have a budget? What items should be included for you personally? What items could you eliminate? What items should you add?

_____

_____

_____

_____

_____

_____

_____

_____

_____

_____

EXERCISES 5-4

Create a budget for yourself. Include your sources of income, as well as your expenses.

INVESTMENTS

SECTION 18

INVESTMENTS

He who ignores discipline comes to poverty and shame,
but whoever heeds correction is honored.
—Proverbs 12:18—

THERE IS A NOTION THAT INVESTMENTS are only in the stock market, but they are dreadfully wrong. An investment can be anything ranging from education, to gold, to stock, to bonds, or to real estate. Investments are a valuable resource for you to generate financial growth and earnings. You should have the assumption that if you effectively investment, you are allowing your money to grow and appreciate in value.

Yes, there is risk to investing, but there is risk to everything in life; driving a car, going to college, or even beginning a career. It is your own personal preference deciding how much you are willing to risk, and how much is too much. But we must look at risk from the other end, with the fact that having no investment at all is risky too. You are losing the chance to grow your money, and create more revenues for yourself, and financial future. Essentially, you are giving up the chance to make free money.

To invest your money successfully, you must have different options of investments (with various risks), and diversify your investments to avoid the complete loss of your funds. Everyone is different, and has a different tolerant of risk than others. We all have our preferences, and have our personal strategies. You just have to decide which is right for you, in terms of your comfort level of risk.

What is right for investors on television or in the magazines may not be right for you. There is an abundance of investing information available to us, and if you try to read it all, you will never have the time to actually make any investments. It is smart to investigate, and research various investing options, but do not try to follow what everyone else does in the market; but make the decisions on your own, based on your thorough study.

Once you figure out *what* to invest, then it is time to move on to creating your portfolio.

PRAYER:

Lord, I ask that you help me avoid the trend of doing what others are doing, and make these investment decisions on my own, with the consult of a selected few. I ask that you help me keep a clear vision, and never let me become greedy when it comes to money, or any other earthly treasures. Amen.

JOURNAL:

Have you ever made any investments? If yes, how did you decide which investments to make? What is your comfort level of risk? What investments interest you?

_____

_____

_____

_____

_____

_____

_____

_____

_____

_____

_____

EXERCISES 6-1

Have you ever made any investments? If yes, how did you decide which investments to make and what is your comfort level of risk?

PORTFOLIO

SECTION 19

PORTFOLIO

A PORTFOLIO IS SIMPLY A NUMERICAL outline to help you know and keep track of where your funds are allocated, and a list of what investments you are engaged in. The key to making a successful portfolio of your finances is to ***diversify!*** Diversify means to invest in various accounts or financial institutions. This is also called asset allocation and diversification. By diversifying your investments, you are essentially lowering the risk.

For example, if you had a diversified portfolio, and the stock market crashed, you would not lose your entire life savings, because you would have investments elsewhere.

The potential return on any investment will be depended upon your risk that you assume on your investment. If you are not willing to have a high level of risk, then you might invest in bonds. It does not yield as high of a percentage of interest, but it is not as risky of an investment in comparison to stocks.

An example of a diversified portfolio outline may be that you have invested:

- 10% in Real Estate
- 20% in Bonds
- 20% in Domestic Stocks
- 10% in Foreign Stocks
- 15% in Mutual Funds
- 25% in Commodities

PRAYER:

Lord, I thank you for the gift of knowledge, and for your guidance. I ask that when I develop a portfolio, you give me the wisdom to make smart choices that are appropriate for me personally. I ask that you help me avoid trying to be like other people, and establish who I am as an investor on my own. Thank you for helping me Lord. Amen.

JOURNAL:

In what ways can you diversify your portfolio? What is your level of risk, and what are you going to invest in to reflect your risk level? Have you researched these various investment opportunities?

_____

_____

_____

_____

_____

_____

_____

_____

_____

_____

EXERCISES 6-2

Create a pie chart to demonstrate the way you plan to diversify your portfolio, and divide your investments into various accounts and funds.

STOCKS

SECTION 20

STOCKS

Prepare your work outside, and make it ready for yourself in the
field; afterwards, then, build your house.
—Proverbs 24:27—

WHEN MOST PEOPLE THINK OF THE WORD investing, stocks and the stock
market may be the first thing that comes to mind. Generally speaking,
investing in stocks offers larger returns than any other investment
opportunity, but there is also more risk involved than any other form of
investment. Stocks are complex, there are a lot of decisions and research
involved with investing in the stock market, and there are thousands of
stocks to choose from. So how do you know which is the best option for
you?

The first step is to do thorough, and in depth research about the
company you are looking to invest in. Look at their past performance,
how did they do in the past five years? What are their dividends they pay
out to their shareholders? What is their company reputation? Just as you
did research about a company for a potential job; you must invest that
same amount of time and effort into making an investment; because it is
real money that you can lose faster than you even realize what's
happening. Look for increasing sales revenues, an increasing net income,
and an increase in the corporation's earnings per share. If these are
prevalent in the company you are inquiring, the information reveals they
are stable, and in a healthy financial position.

In the long term, the average stock will grow about 10-12% a year, fluctuating on a monthly and yearly basis. This is just a simple way to monitor your stocks, and see how well they are performing.

There are two types of stocks; common stock and preferred stock. We will examine the two types in this next section.

Common Stock: Common stockholders are the actual owners of the organization. They make their money from the investment two ways: income from the dividends and dollar appreciation of stock value.

Preferred Stock: With a preferred stock investment, the investor would receive cash dividends before the common stockholders are paid any cash dividends. The dividend on the preferred stock is known before you even purchase the stock, whereas the common stock receives an unknown dividend. This option lacks the growth potential that the common stocks offer.

The internet has made it easier than ever to buy and sell stocks. Stock brokers used to be the sole way to be active in the stock market, but now with sites such as E*TRADE and Scottrade; investment is made easy, and accessible. These are the sites that have low trade rates, while striving to be user friendly and easy for a beginning investor.

- https://us.etrade.com/e/t/home ($8-10 for an online trade)
- http://www.scottrade.com/ ($7 for an online trade)
- http://www.moolanomy.com/1644/online-discount-stock-brokers/ (Gives the lowest rates for online trading, and what each site provides and charges)

PRAYER:

Lord, I thank you for the opportunity to invest my money, and allow it to grow. I ask that you help me be a good steward of this money, and never become greedy, or lustful. Keep me humble, and glorify you in all situations, and blessings. Amen.

JOURNAL:

What companies interest you? What companies do you think will grow in the future? How would you diversify your stock investments?

_____

_____

_____

_____

_____

_____

_____

_____

_____

_____

_____

_____

EXERCISES 6-3

Research five companies that interest you and could be a potential investment. What are your findings? What stocks would you buy, and why?

BONDS

SECTIONS 21

BONDS

BONDS HAVE ALWAYS BEEN CONSIDERED a safe investment, especially in complex economic times. When the stock market seems unstable, bonds are more attractive to invest in. Keeping a diversified portfolio is key to reducing risk, and ensuring a balanced portfolio of investments.

Corporate bonds are common when investors want a safe investing option. A corporate bond is similar to a reverse loan, where a company creates a written pledge to repay a specific amount of money with interest back to you within the maturity date (date on which the company must repay the borrowed money).

Corporations sell these bonds for a variety of reasons and purposes. They sell these bonds when:

- They do not have enough money to make payments on large purchases/expansions
- They need extra money to finance business activities
- They find it hard to sell stock
- They want to improve their financial leverage
- Or when they use the interest paid to the bond owners as a tax-deducible expense which reduces how much they must pay the federal government

You can also purchase bonds from the United States Treasury; which has a lower return, but less risk involved. The government uses five types of securities:

1. **Treasury Bills**
   a. T-Bill, discounted securities with the purchase price being less than the maturity value.

2. **Treasury Bonds**
   a. Issued in $100 units, with maturity date of 30 years. Can receive interest payments every six months.

3. **Treasury Notes**
   a. Also called a T-Note, is issued in $100 units, with a maturity time of two, five, or 10 years. This investment yields a higher return than the T-bill because it is a longer investment.

4. **Treasury Inflation-Protected Securities**
   a. Also called TIPS, are sold with $100 units, and have a maturity of five, 10 or 20 years. The principal increases with inflation, and decreases with deflation.

5. **United States Government Savings Bonds**
   a. These bonds increase every month, and interest compounds semi annually. May be exempt from interest tax and you do not have to pay federal income tax on earnings until the bond is redeemed.

For more information, and rates for the government sponsored bonds; go to **www.treasurydirect.gov**.

PRAYER:

Lord, I thank you for the chance to invest, but need clarity in the various forms of investing. Please show me what investment is right, and wise of me; while ensuring stability in my financial future. Thank you for providing me with the luxury of investing; and for growing my portfolio through these various investments. Amen.

JOURNAL:

Have you ever worked with bonds? What types of bonds seem attractive to you? How long are you willing to invest your money into bonds? What is the rate you desire from bonds or other investments?

_____

_____

_____

_____

_____

_____

_____

_____

_____

_____

_____

EXERCISES 6-4

Research the rates for government bonds, which type of bond seems to be the best option? How long do you want your money to be "tied up," into that specific bond?

MUTUAL FUNDS

SECTION 22

MUTUAL FUNDS

WHEN YOU WANT A RETURN on your investment, but don't have a high tolerance of risk, a mutual fund may be the best option for you. A mutual fund is an investment company that combines the money of investors (its shareholders), to invest in a variety of securities.

The major reason investors put their money into mutual funds is the fact that it is professionally managed, and diversified. Its performance is based on the collective results from various companies, providing less risk.

There are three different mutual funds that are common today:

1. **Closed-End Funds**
   a. Shares are issued by an investment company only when the fund is organized. Only a specified number of shares are available to the investor. Actively managed by a professional and the price is determined by the demand, similar to the stock market.

2. **Exchange-Traded Fund**
   a. Invests in stocks or other securities contained in a specific stock or securities index. Less management from professionals, and stocks in specific index. This mutual fund is similar to the stock market, and mirrors overall performance.

3. **Open-Ended Funds**
   a. The shares are issued and redeemed at the request of the investor by the investment company. The investors can buy and sell these shares at the net asset value (NAV).

Mutual funds give you a third investment option that is lower returns, but also less risky. This is a fitting option for someone that wants a diversified portfolio, but is still concerned about the risk.

PRAYER:

Lord, thank you, I am so blessed to live in a place that gives me the freedom of investing my money, and the control over how much to save and tithe. Please help me maintain a giving heart, no matter where I am at in my financial journey. Amen.

JOURNAL:

What are your thoughts on mutual funds? Do you see yourself investing in these funds in the future? What kind of risk are you willing to take?

_____

_____

_____

_____

_____

_____

_____

_____

_____

_____

_____

_____

_____

_____

_____

_____

EXERCISES 6-5

Research the rates for government bonds, which type of bond seems to be the best option? How long do you want your money to be "tied up," into that specific bond?

REAL ESTATE

SECTION 23

REAL ESTATE

By wisdom a house is built,
and by understanding it is established;
and by knowledge the rooms are filled
with all precious and pleasant riches.
—Proverbs 24:3-4—

LOCATION. LOCATION. LOCATION. We have all heard this common phrase when dealing with business real estate, but it also applies to your home. Making an investment in real estate brings up many decisions you must make; to buy? To rent? To invest? It is going to be different for everyone, so it depends on your finances and personal preference.

For the longest time, real estate has said to have been the "safe haven" for investors, because it has had a constant return on investment (ROI). But in the recent years, with the housing bubble crisis and an all-time high on foreclosures, real-estate is not as safe as it used to be.

Renters receive short term benefits off of their investment while homeowners reap a longer term investment with long-term returns and solutions. Each form of real estate has their risks, as well as pros and cons; but the main purpose is to find a home dwelling that is right for you. You need to decide whether you should buy or rent; or if you should invest or keep away.

Some advantages and disadvantages of **buying a home** are (and not limited to):

ADVANTAGES	DISADVANTAGES
Hedge against inflation	Large Financial Commitment
Pride of Ownership	Lack of diversification
You will have financial leverage	Higher living expenses than renting
Tax Incentives	Higher maintenance responsibilities

Some advantages and disadvantages of **renting an apartment or home** are (and not limited to):

ADVANTAGES	DISADVANTAGES
Easy to Move	No tax benefits
Fewer Responsibilities for Maintenance	Limitations regarding remodeling
Minimal Financial Commitment	Restrictions regarding pets, etc.
Not responsible for depreciation	Lack of space

Before buying or renting a home (or apartment), it is crucial you thoroughly evaluate what you can afford, and what size or quality is essential for your lifestyle. You do not want to buy something that is above your means, and financial capability; or you will suffer long-term financial stress. You should evaluate where you work, how much you are making, and have the potential of making, in addition to the consideration of moving for a different position or job. In this market, it is not as easy to sell a house as it used to be, which means how important it is to wait to buy a home until you are at a secured point in your life.

For example, if the market is not stable, and you do not have the funds for the full down payment, it will be a smarter option to rent until you save enough to afford the down payment on a home. Or, if you are at a steady point in your career, you are settled down and have the funds to make a down payment, then buying a home may be a good option for you. Just realize the costs that are associated with purchasing and maintaining a home; you not only have a significant down payment, but there are a lot of maintenance costs, property taxes, the risk of market fluctuation, wear/tear on your house, and insurance that is associated with home buying.

Mortgages

To pay for your home, you will most likely take out a mortgage, which is a long-term loan on the specific property and real estate. This long term loan will usually last for 10, 15, 20, or even 30 years; and is given by banks, credit unions, loan associations or loan companies. There are also mortgage brokers who help potential home owners obtain financing through their contacts at various financial institutions, but charge higher fees than a lending source because of their contacts.

To qualify for a mortgage, there are many qualifications and criteria you must meet to be granted the mortgage, such as credit score, or your leverage in case you are not able to make payments. Your home you buy will also be used as leverage for the mortgage you take out. Remember that the faster you pay the mortgage, the less interest you pay, and the quicker you are able to enjoy the freedom from the high-interest mortgage.

A method to figure out what your monthly payments could be as follows:

1. Determine your monthly gross income.
2. With a down payment of at least 3%, lenders use 33% of monthly gross income as guidelines for PITI (Principal, interest, taxes and insurance) or 38% of monthly gross income if you have a mortgage and other debts.

3. Subtract other debt payments and an estimate of monthly costs of property taxes and homeowner's insurance.
   THIS GIVES YOU YOUR AFFORDABLE MONTHLY MORTGAGE PAYMENT

So, after reading this, do you think real estate is truly a safe haven for investors?? The answer is NO! Similar to any other investment, there will be risks. There will be fluctuations in the market that are unforeseen and other changes that may affect your real estate investment.

PRAYER:

Lord, thank you for your gifts and treasures on earth. I ask that through this process of buying or renting a home that you give me wisdom and discipline to choose an option that is right for me, for the place I am at in my life. Thank you for always providing, and for teaching me self control to not desire things I cannot afford, and do not need. Amen.

JOURNAL:

Do you know what components of a house/apartment you want? What do you consider a necessity when choosing a home dwelling? Would you rather rent for longer and buy a more expensive home, or vice versa? When shopping for a home, be firm in your budget and price range.

_____

_____

_____

_____

_____

_____

_____

_____

EXERCISES 6-6

When you graduate, where do you want to live? Do you want to buy or rent? Create a list of musts, and wants; and recognize the difference of priority when shopping for a home or apartment. Find two houses/apartments that would be within your means to rent/buy.

CAREER PLAN

SECTION 24

CAREER PLAN

"Whatever you do, work at it with all your heart, as working for the
Lord, not for men, since you know that you will receive inheritance
from the Lord as a reward. It is the Lord Christ you are serving."
—Colossians 3:23-24—

I AM SURE YOU ARE familiar with the question, "so what are you going to
do after graduation?" Many individuals are unsure about their immediate
plans for a job out of college, but they may have their career plan figured
out. The main difference between a job and a career is the time they take
place in. A job it short term, and a career is a long term plan for your
vocation. Jobs give you a short term form of income, while a career is
related to your long term goal and looking at the final destination of
where you want to be vocationally.

Everyone's career plan will be different; focusing on specific industries,
and salaries that relate to your pursued field. Based on your dream job,
your job direction, and positions will be different to fulfill your personal
career goals. It is important to recognize that some careers are becoming
obsolete, and you may not want to continue your career plan, if you can
foresee this happening in the future to your vocation. Technology has
replaced travel agents with an online travel network, bank tellers with
ATM's, cashiers at grocery stores with self-checkout lanes, stock brokers
are being replaced with online trading sites (E*TRADE, Scott Trade, etc),
logistic managers are being replaced by teleconferencing, mail carriers are
being replaced by email, and other electronic ways to send messages, and
even some teachers are being replaced by online, and virtual classrooms.

When mapping out your career plan, figure out how much education you need. To progress, and advance, do you have to earn your Masters, or completion of a Graduate Program? Understand these qualifications, and plan your finances accordingly. This also may include your skills, and expertise. What skills do you need to develop to be promoted within your company?

No matter what your career plan may be, you must be committed to continually growing, and developing as a person, and employee. In a world that is changing on a daily basis, you must make yourself valuable, and needed, no matter what changes in the world. By always developing, you are staying competitive in your field, while creating distinctive competencies for yourself that no one else may have. You also must be aware of the salary for the entrance level position, as well as the salary for those with experience, and precedence. This will help you map out your financial plan, as well as be realistic when negotiating.

Find a mentor in your field that would be willing to share what you need to do to get promoted, and how you can stand out in your specific industry. Find out what skills you need to develop to the employee of your potential. This will also reveal the "insider" information about the job, and give you an idea of the pros and cons; and if this is truly the career plan you want to embark on.

A final step to forming your career plan is to explore the international/global opportunities within your field, and determine what their global competition or growth opportunity will be in the future? How will the competition of other countries affect your field? Can you be competitive with foreign countries? Are there any partnerships that you foresee in the future on a global scale? How much travel could be required? In response to these questions, you have to make some decisions with your willingness to be involved with this global market, and how it will affect your future. Are you willing to travel frequently? Will it require you to be gone for weeks at a time? Will you enjoy this when you are married? Will you enjoy this when you have children? Will the travel allow you enough time to sustain a household?

These are all questions you must consider when forming your career plan; because if you are unsure if you can give the time/travel that the company needs, you may never reach that dream position. Don't be discouraged if you are unsure of your career plan, this is the time to be considering these questions, and figuring out what kind of life you want to live; and what you are willing to sacrifice to achieve that position.

PRAYER:

Lord, I thank you for the passions you have given me to begin my career journey, but I ask that you be with me in every step when making these decisions. Help me become the man/woman you have made me to be; and open my eyes to the career you have designed me to obtain. Amen.

JOURNAL:

What is your dream job? Where do you see your career in 15 years? What kinds of benefits do you want? Do you want a family, and if so, will travel be possible? What education and skills do you need to obtain to continue developing as an employee and person?

_____

_____

_____

_____

_____

_____

_____

_____

_____

_____

EXERCISES 7-1

What is your dream job? Where do you see your career in 15 years? Make a career plan with attainable steps to reach your dream job.

EDUCATION

SECTION 25

EDUCATION

EDUCATION IN ESSENCE IS A LIFELONG journey, and we must always desire to learn more. With that being said, if education is a lifelong journey, then it could get very expensive. Education is a form of investment. Although people say you can't put a price on education, it is wise to make sure the returns on your educational investment are great enough. You must know how much your education will cost you, and what the return will be, because education often leads people into extreme debt, that traps them of their financial freedom. It is best to find out exactly what you want to do, and study early in your educational journey, to utilize your time, and funds to focus in one key area (and to finish on time). By discerning your field of expertise early on, you also avoid unnecessary education, and debt.

Education does not only take the form of a classroom, but you can receive education through other associates, through internships and jobs, training seminars, or earning a college certificate. The more knowledge you have, the more money you make, by having more expertise, you are able to consider yourself at a higher value than others, and in turn; make more. But be careful with how much you pay in education, because if you are spending over $100,000, and your job only earns $17,000, you may want to consider other options.

PRAYER:

Lord, I thank you for providing the funds to make my education affordable, but most of all, I thank you for allowing me to learn every day about Your love and grace. Thank you God for teaching me Your ways, and allowing me to grow, and learn from my mistakes along the way. I ask that you help me make the most of my time here, and help me persevere when it gets hard. Amen.

JOURNAL:

What is your view on education? What goals do you have for your college experience? What are you going to do to make these the best years of your life, filled with growth, maturity, and lifelong relationships?

_____

_____

_____

_____

_____

_____

_____

_____

_____

_____

_____

EXERCISES 7-2

What level of education is required for your position? Make an education layout of what is required (if any) to get a promotion/advancement.

EMERGENCY PLANS

SECTION 26

EMERGENCY PLANS

The plans of the diligent lead surely to advantage,
but everyone who is hasty surely to poverty.
—Proverbs 21:5—

IT IS VITALLY IMPORTANT TO THINK through emergency plans, and how you will respond to certain unfortunate incidents in your life. A few reasons/circumstances that might affect your financial plan, and force you to take funds from your savings include:

- Loss of Job
- Demotion
- Death of main financial provider
- Sufficient medical bills from unexpected tragedy
- Car accident
- Serious Health Problems
- Emergency Room Care
- Illnesses
- Extended care
- Sever Injury

With the examples demonstrated in this list, and what you will learn in this financial plan, you will have fully realized the importance of creating and maintaining an emergency plan with emergency funds.

With all this in mind; it is important when saving, to not only invest in the market, and save for the future (retirement); but also save for an emergency fund so you are able to live in assurance knowing you are prepared for whatever comes your way.

PRAYER:

Lord, I thank you for your blessings in my life, and knowing that you make all things work together for my good. Lord, I know bad things happen to good people, and I know it is always for a reason, and for your greater plan for my life. Thank you for preparing me for anything that may come my way. Amen.

JOURNAL:

Have you ever experienced an emergency in which you had to give up your savings for? What would you do if you didn't have any savings for this?

_____

_____

_____

_____

_____

_____

_____

_____

_____

_____

_____

_____

_____

_____

_____

_____

Exercises 7-3

Have you ever experienced an unexpected event that impacted your source of income? How did you respond? To properly prepare for the future, make a plan to save extra money for an emergency fund.

ROAD MAP

SECTION 27

ROAD MAP

"For I know the plans I have for you," declares the Lord, "plans to prosper you and not to harm you, plans to give you hope and a future. Then you will call upon me and come and pray to me, and I will listen to you. You will seek me and find me when you see me with all your heart. I will be found by you," declares the Lord, "and will bring you back from captivity."
—Jeremiah 29:11-14—

THIS FINANCIAL PLAN IS DESIGNED to help you, and to teach you how to develop an effective financial strategy. The key to a successful plan is to begin today, and make your initiatives and goals realistic, measurable, and achievable. You should make a vision board, and create your road map. Where are you at now, where do you see yourself in 5 years? 10 years? 50 years?

What financial goals are you committing to, and what steps are you taking to achieve them? What road blocks and hardships do you foresee? What is your motivation to stay on course and achieve your plan?

At this point, create a road map to give you a visual direction of where you want your life to go. Understand that God has the ultimate plan, and His plans are far greater than anything we can imagine; but proper preparation is still essential.

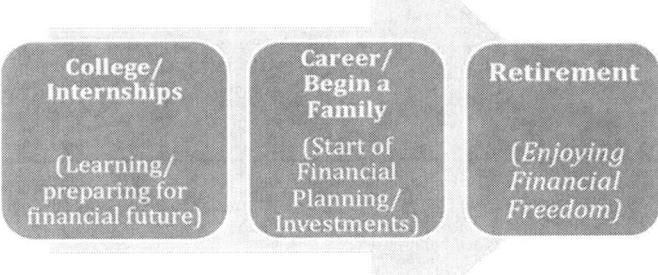

PRAYER:

Lord, I ask that you guide me, and help me follow your will and plan for my life. Lord, I ask that you help me use this road map not as an absolute, but as a way to be diligent and meticulous in my devotion to a promising financial future. Thank you for staying by my side. Amen.

JOURNAL:

Where are you at now? Where do you want to go? What major events do you have to achieve to get to your destination?

_____
_____
_____
_____
_____
_____
_____
_____
_____
_____

EXERCISES 7-4

Create a road map of your future plans/stages. Include major chapters in your life. Use the space below as your vision board:

CONCLUSION

SECTION 28

CONCLUSION

Don't let anyone look down on you because you are young, but set
an example for believers in speech, in life, in love, in faith and in
purity. Until I come, devote yourself to the public reading of
Scripture, to preaching and teaching. Do not neglect your gift that
was given to you through a prophetic message when the body of
elders laid their hands on you.
—1 Timothy 4:12-14—

THROUGH PERSONAL FINANCE, YOU not only gain perspective about the
rewards and success that comes from proper planning, but also the
knowledge and wisdom to live a life of financial stability.

If you utilize this information, and take advantage of your personal
financial plan you will have a jumpstart on your journey for financial
abundance. I challenge you to not look at this personal financial plan as
something that you just have to get through; but look at it as a vital
resource for your future, and learning how to use the blessings that God
has provided, and live a stress free life of giving, and making an impact.

PRAYER:

Lord, I ask that you be with me as I embark on this journey, and let me
remember this knowledge and wisdom for my future. Allow me to be a
good steward of your money, and to use my blessings to further your
kingdom and purpose. Thank you for giving me the financial freedom to
follow my dreams, passions, and purpose. Amen.

JOURNAL:

What have you changed to begin your financial journey? How dedicated are you to following though with your financial plan after reading this book?

_____

_____

_____

_____

_____

_____

_____

_____

_____

_____

_____

_____

EXERCISES 7-5:

Create a one page (400 words) summary of the top 5 most valuable lessons you have gained through this personal financial plan.

ABOUT THE AUTHOR

VILMA EDGINTON holds a Ph.D. in Economics and Politics from the Claremont Graduate University, Claremont, CA. She also holds an MBA, Masters of Business Administration degree from Wayne State University, Detroit, Michigan. She obtained her Bachelor of Arts from the University of Guelph, Guelph, Ontario, Canada.

Vilma is an economist for the jewelry and diamond industries. She also consults with medium-large privately held jewelry companies both domestically and internationally. Prior to her affiliation with the jewelry and diamond industries, Mrs. Edginton was an economist for Wachovia Securities in San Diego, CA.

She enjoy spending time with her family, hiking and some mountain biking. She also enjoy reading to her wonderful nephews and niece, taking long walks with her father, and cooking over-the-top meals with her amazing mother! She is also thinking of adding scrapbooking to her list of hobbies since both her sisters produce perfect scrapbook cards. And lastly, she enjoys morning, afternoon, and evening café lattés with her husband.

CPSIA information can be obtained at www.ICGtesting.com
Printed in the USA
LVOW09s1214181015

458745LV00020B/505/P